Conflict
Therapy

CW00740848

Conflict Resolution Therapy

written by
Juliette Garesché

illustrated by
R.W. Alley

Abbey Press

Text © 2010 by Juliette Garesché
Illustrations © 2010 by St. Meinrad Archabbey
Published by One Caring Place
Abbey Press
St. Meinrad, Indiana 47577

Library of Congress Control Number
2009910934

ISBN 978-0-87029-430-3

Printed in the United States of America

Foreword

If we lived alone in the world, we wouldn't face conflict. But we were created to be in community. And it is often with those individuals we love the most, that we have the most heated conflict. When another person has a point of view that doesn't make sense to us, it can be upsetting, confusing, and even threatening. It is good to be aware of your emotions, and the other person's emotions, as you work through these differences of opinion.

When conflict does arise, it can be a struggle to find common ground. *Conflict Resolution Therapy* defines some basic skills to use as we respectfully listen to one another's perspectives and work toward mutually beneficial solutions to our problems. If we know how to deal with conflict constructively, we can come out of these discussions stronger, and with a deepened sense of trust.

Good luck, God's blessings, and peace to you and your household.

1.

Conflicts are a normal, unavoidable part of life. They occur when opinions or priorities differ between people. Throughout our lives we will encounter people who see things differently than we do. That's OK. That's what makes life interesting!

2.

Some people actually welcome conflict as an opportunity to expand their ideas and to learn something new!

3.

If mismanaged, conflict can erupt into a battle of wills, a matter of who is right and who is wrong. This is very hard on you and those around you.

4.

If conflict isn't handled properly, it may also lead to frequent arguments and misery. That's why it is **so** important that we learn how to manage conflict.

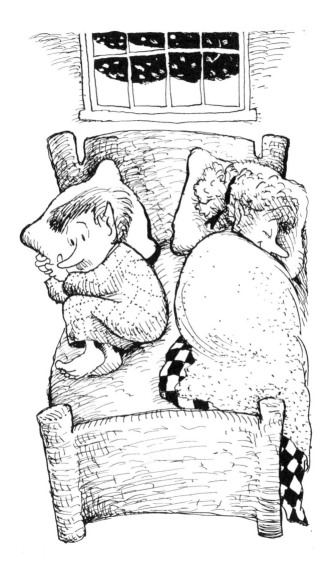

5.

Most people can work out a difference of opinion if only one person is upset. It is much harder to resolve a situation where two people are upset with each other.

6.

If one or both parties are upset, take a break. No one can solve a problem when they are angry or feel threatened.

7.

When we are upset, blood flow decreases to the front part of our brains, the very area that helps us come up with creative solutions!

8.

Wait until you both have calmed down and you feel rational and ready to work through the situation. It may take five minutes or half a day.

9.

Think about calming strategies before you are in a conflict. Do you calm down best when you take a walk, pray, talk to a friend, or squeeze a stress ball?

10.

It isn't helpful to ignore disagreements. You may feel like withdrawing by watching TV, going to sleep, or trying to forget about the whole problem. This is called "stuffing" your feelings; it's <u>not</u> a good long-term solution to conflict.

11.

Talk through your feelings until you reach an agreement both parties can live with. When you take the time to work through a disagreement until both parties are happy, it shows you care about the other person's happiness too.

12.

Avoid "communication fouls" such as: name calling, blaming, yelling, cursing, interrupting, or disrespect. Stick to talking about the current situation; don't dredge up the past.

13.

Take turns talking. Imagine that you are a "container" and let the other person be the "speaker." "Containers" don't talk (yet) so try not to formulate a response to what the "speaker" is saying.

14.

As the "container," practice your very best **active** listening. It is the "container's" job to hold all of the words, opinions, and feelings of the "speaker."

15.

When the "speaker" has finished, summarize what you heard them say. Don't insert your own thoughts. Let them know you listened carefully and you understand **their** point of view.

16.

The "speaker" may then confirm whether or not you captured all of their main points. If you missed something, the "speaker" will re-clarify. Make a point of listening extra carefully.

17.

This may seem a slow process, but there is great healing in knowing that another person is taking the time to understand you. During the process, you may notice their tension drain away.

18.

Another technique is using an "I statement." These include your feelings and when the emotion is present for you. For example, "<u>I feel</u> sad <u>when</u> I'm not invited to join you." Or, "<u>I feel</u> mad <u>when</u> my things are broken."

19.

Words ending with "ed" such as embarrassed, offended, belittled, or disrespected are not feelings. They make the "container" feel he or she is being blamed and it could break down positive communication.

20.

Anger, a common emotion during conflict, is a **secondary emotion**. It covers up more tender, vulnerable feelings such as fear, loneliness, hurt, or disappointment.

21.

Consider anger as a red flag, telling you to search inwardly for the tender feeling behind the anger. Understand where the feeling may come from and why it is surfacing now.

22.

Own your feelings. You may feel vulnerable sharing your feelings, but that is the only way others can understand how you are feeling. It is a wonderful way to build intimacy in a relationship.

23.

Don't assume you know how someone else feels. You can only know for sure if they tell you. The exact same situation can elicit completely opposite feelings from two individuals.

24.

Once you know that you heard the other person's point of view and feelings correctly, change roles. Now it is your turn to be the "speaker" and they will be the "container."

25.

Take turns talking about what each person wants in order to make the situation better. Do you want an apology? Money to replace something that was lost or broken? Chores to be divided more fairly? Express it.

26.

Recognize that disagreements often arise with those nearest to us. The day-to-day overlap of space and schedules can be a breeding ground for conflict. Small, everyday problems can grow into bigger issues, so it's especially important to address them with care and consideration.

27.

Be willing to compromise to make the situation better for both people. If your spouse, child, friend, or colleague is important to you, let them know! The solutions you come up with can be as creative and original as the two of you.

28.

Remember that each person may have their own favorite way of feeling better. Take time to really assess what will make you feel better.

29.

It may be important for your husband to hear an apology or the words "I love you," but your child may want your time or attention. Be open, try new things, and respect their wishes.

30.

There is an art to apologizing.
Most people aren't impressed
with a shrug and a quick,
"Sorry."

31.

When apologizing, use eye contact, call the person by name, and tell them specifically what you are sorry for having done. Tell them what you'll do to make it better and how you'll handle that type of situation differently in the future.

32.

Understand the difference between dialogue and debate. Debate is a form of competition designed to persuade others to see your point of view only. It is designed to have a winner and a loser.

33.

Dialogue is a way of sharing thoughts that looks for an overlap of ideas and for common ground. When you're looking for a mutual resolution, which method do you think will be most effective?

34.

If you get stuck in a conflict, try calling in a third person to help mediate your disagreement. A parent, a pastor, or another mature person may help you to see solutions you never thought of before.

35.

You are never alone in a conflict. You can take any conflict to God in prayer and ask that both your hearts be softened so you are willing to compromise and accommodate one another.

36.

Forgiveness can play an important role in letting go of big hurts. God can help you with this too.

37.

Let those who witnessed your conflict know when you've worked it out. When parents let their children know they've worked through a disagreement, they are modeling effective communication skills and good conflict resolution skills for their children.

38.

The more you practice these new skills, the more easily and naturally you will glide through the process. May you find peace in your home and relationships as you work through the conflicts that life brings to us all!

Juliette Garesché helped to found *Peace Learning Circles,* a non-profit organization that teaches conflict resolution skills to children. She is the author of *Learning About Virtues,* also published by Abbey Press. She lives with her son in Kenosha, Wisconsin.

Illustrator for the Abbey Press Elf-help Books, **R.W. Alley** also illustrates and writes children's books. He lives in Barrington, Rhode Island, with his wife, daughter, and son. See a wide variety of his works at: www.rwalley.com.

The Story of the Abbey Press Elves

The engaging figures that populate the Abbey Press "elf-help" line of publications and products first appeared in 1987 on the pages of a small self-help book called *Be-good-to-yourself Therapy*. Shaped by the publishing staff's vision and defined in R.W. Alley's inventive illustrations, they lived out author Cherry Hartman's gentle, self-nurturing advice with charm, poignancy, and humor.

Reader response was so enthusiastic that more Elf-help Books were soon under way, a still-growing series that has inspired a line of related gift products.

The especially endearing character featured in the early books—sporting a cap with a mood-changing candle in its peak—has since been joined by a spirited female elf with flowers in her hair.

These two exuberant, sensitive, resourceful, kindhearted, lovable sprites, along with their lively elfin community, reveal what's truly important as they offer messages of joy and wonder, playfulness and co-creation, wholeness and serenity, the miracle of life and the mystery of God's love.

With wisdom and whimsy, these little creatures with long noses demonstrate the elf-help way to a rich and fulfilling life.

Elf-help Books

...adding "a little character" and a lot
of help to self-help reading!

Friendship Therapy	#20174
Christmas Therapy (color edition) $5.95	#20175
Happy Birthday Therapy	#20181
Forgiveness Therapy	#20184
Keep-life-simple Therapy	#20185
Acceptance Therapy	#20190
Keeping-up-your-spirits Therapy	#20195
Slow-down Therapy	#20203
One-day-at-a-time Therapy	#20204
Prayer Therapy	#20206
Be-good-to-your-marriage Therapy	#20205
Be-good-to-yourself Therapy	#20255

Book price is $4.95 unless otherwise noted.
Available at your favorite gift shop or bookstore—
or directly from One Caring Place, Abbey Press
Publications, St. Meinrad, IN 47577.
Or call 1-800-325-2511.
www.carenotes.com